SEE IN 3-D

POLAR ANIMALS

SEYMOUR SIMON

SCHOLASTIC INC.
New York Toronto London Auckland Sydney
Mexico City New Delhi Hong Kong Buenos Aires

To Wendy Schmalz,
with many thanks for being my agent
and appreciation for being my friend.

ACKNOWLEDGMENTS

Special thanks to Ron Labbe of Studio 3D for his expertise and 3D photo conversions. Thanks also to Alison Kolani for her skillful copyediting. The author is grateful to David Reuther and Ellen Friedman for their editorial and design suggestions, as well as their enthusiasm for this project. Also, many thanks to Gina Shaw, Suzanne Nelson, and Carla Siegel at Scholastic Inc., for their generous help and support.

PHOTO CREDITS

Front cover: © Konrad Wothe/Science Faction Images/Getty Images; back cover: © Gerard Lacz/Animals-Animals; pages 1, 4: © Wayne R. Bilenduke/Getty Images; page 3: © Joseph Van Os/Getty Images; pages 6–7: © Mary Clay/Dembinsky Photo Associates; page 8: © Norbert Rosing/Getty Images; page 9: © Tom McHugh/Photo Researchers, Inc.; pages 10–11: © Thomas & Pat Leeson/Photo Researchers, Inc.; page 13: © Michael Giannechini/Photo Researchers, Inc.; pages 14–15: © Jasmine Rossi/SeaPics.com; page 16: © Frank Lukasseck/zefa/Corbis; page 17: © Jan Tove Johansson/Getty Images; pages 18–19: © Tim Davis/Corbis; page 20: © Tom Tietz/Getty Images; page 21: © Digital Vision/Getty Images; pages 22–23: © 3D Vision International; page 24: © Johnny Johnson/Getty Images.

ISBN-13: 978-0-439-86650-7
ISBN-10: 0-439-86650-2

12 11 10 9 8 7 6 5 4 3   9 10 11 12/0

Printed in the U.S.A.
First printing, January 2007

Imagine a place where temperatures can reach -50°
Fahrenheit (-45° Celsius) and fierce winds blow across
endless fields of ice and snow. This is winter in the Arctic
and Antarctic. Nothing seems to be alive. Yet, even during the
coldest months, some animals, such as Arctic wolves and foxes,
musk oxen, caribou, and snowy owls, are out searching for
food. Other animals, such as female polar bears and ground
squirrels, sleep the winter away in dens beneath the snow.

Male polar bears are the largest meat-eaters living on land. They can grow to be 11 feet long and can weigh over 1,500 pounds. Their strong paws have very sharp claws and are nearly a foot across. Polar bears also have powerful jaws. They use their 42 sharp teeth to tear food apart.

Their huge feet allow polar bears to run easily over ice and snow. The bears are also good swimmers, but they are no match for seals in the water. They catch seals by silently stalking them on the ice. When they are within striking distance, they attack with blows from their huge paws. Then the polar bears settle down for their meal.

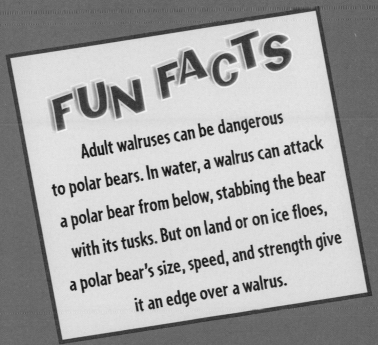

FUN FACTS

Adult walruses can be dangerous to polar bears. In water, a walrus can attack a polar bear from below, stabbing the bear with its tusks. But on land or on ice floes, a polar bear's size, speed, and strength give it an edge over a walrus.

The Arctic wolf is a close cousin of the gray wolves that live farther south. But the Arctic wolf is whiter and has a slightly smaller nose and ears than the gray wolf. Roaming alone or in small packs, these wolves hunt over most of Canada's Arctic region and the northern and eastern shores of Greenland.

A large wolf can kill an adult caribou with a crushing bite to the neck. Wolves also hunt together in packs. They usually attack young, old, or sick caribou and musk oxen because they are slower and weaker targets. The wolves also eat small rodents such as lemmings, hares, and ground squirrels.

The Arctic fox has a thick, warm, white coat during the winter and a gray or blue-brown coat in the summer. Its footpads are heavily furred, so the fox travels easily on snow and ice. It feeds on small mammals such as lemmings and voles, birds and bird eggs, berries, and fish. When food is scarce, the fox follows polar bears, hoping to eat the bears' leftover kill. The fox has to be very clever and quick. Otherwise, it might become a polar bear's lunch.

Lemmings are small rodents that live in Norway. They look like hamsters or fat mice. Some years there aren't very many lemmings. But every four years, the snowy fields seem to be alive with the scurrying little animals. And then something very strange happens. The lemmings move across the land in a journey down to the distant sea. When they reach the icy waters, the lemmings plunge in. But they cannot swim across the wide ocean, so thousands and thousands of lemmings drown. The lemmings are trying to escape the crowds of other lemmings by swimming away. In this way, the lemming population never gets too big.

Musk oxen have long, chocolate-brown hair that falls to their hooves. Under the hair, a thick layer of wool protects the animals against frigid winter temperatures.

Musk oxen feed on grasses and other low-growing plants. During the winter, they barely find enough food to survive. The musk oxen lose weight as they live on stored reserves of fat in their bodies.

The musk oxen's only natural enemies are bands of wolves. When wolves appear, the musk oxen form a tight circle. The calves and cows stay at the center of the circle, and the bulls stand shoulder to shoulder around the outside. Their horns point out in every direction. Few wolves will dare to attack a ring of musk oxen.

Caribou are wild reindeer that live mostly in Greenland and northwestern Canada. Their bodies are covered with a thick coat of hair. Each hair is a hollow tube of air. These air spaces trap the caribou's body heat. Their fur gives caribou the best insulation of any mammal in the world.

During the winter, caribou live in herds of up to 100 animals. They use their front feet to dig through snow to uncover the grasses they eat. In the early spring, caribou gather in much larger herds and travel northward. Calves are born along the trip and travel with the herd. Fast-moving herds are able to outdistance packs of wolves. Only weak or sick animals are lost to the packs.

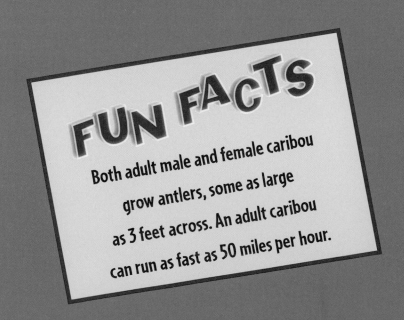

FUN FACTS

Both adult male and female caribou grow antlers, some as large as 3 feet across. An adult caribou can run as fast as 50 miles per hour.

Killer whales, or orcas, are not really whales at all. They're the largest member of the dolphin family. A male can grow to about the length of a school bus and weigh as much as three or four elephants. Orcas live in all the oceans, but most live in the cold waters of the Arctic and Antarctic. Orcas hunt in pods of about 5 to 50 individuals. They eat seals, sea lions, fish, squid, and penguins. They can even attack and kill much larger baleen whales. Yet orcas have not been known to kill people in the wild.

Humpback, gray, and blue whales are baleen whales. They are the largest whales in the world, yet they feed mostly on very small sea animals called krill. Krill are a kind of shrimp no bigger than your little finger. Krill live in huge numbers in Antarctic waters. A baleen whale can swallow two tons of krill in a day.

Seals and walruses are mammals. They breathe air, but they spend most of their lives swimming and eating fish and other small sea animals in the water. They also spend time on land, where they sunbathe and rest and where the mothers give birth.

The Weddell seal lives in the cold water and on the icy shores of Antarctica. It grows up to 10 feet long—that's the height of a basketball hoop. This seal can dive to depths of over 2,000 feet. It can stay underwater for an hour before it comes up for air.

Walruses live in the Arctic and are even bigger than seals.
An adult male walrus weighs about two tons, the same as an
Indian elephant. The first thing you notice about a walrus
is its tusks. Tusks are huge canine teeth that are made of ivory.
They grow to be 2 feet long in females and 4 feet long in males.
Walruses mainly eat clams, snails, shrimp, and worms.

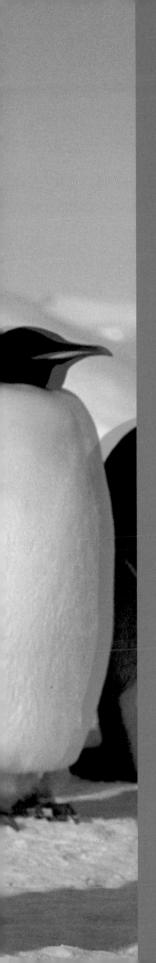

Emperor penguins are the largest penguins in the world. They are almost 4 feet tall and weigh up to 65 pounds. As winter begins in Antarctica, Emperors move inland, traveling as far as 60 miles from the shore. At their breeding grounds, the birds find their mates. In May or June, each female lays a single egg. To keep the egg from freezing on the ice, Emperors balance it on their feet while keeping their body over the egg like a warm blanket.

As soon as the egg is laid, the female heads for the distant open sea. The male protects the egg and keeps it warm for two months while the female is away. The males huddle together in large groups to stay warm during the fierce Antarctic snowstorms, the most violent on Earth. Females return when the eggs are hatching, and the males leave to go to the sea to eat. After three or four weeks, the males return to help feed the chicks.

Puffins live in huge colonies along the icy Arctic shores. These small birds have thick, heavy, waterproof feathers that protect them from the cold. Puffins also have huge bills that store the fish they catch while they hunt underwater.

In breeding season, the parents dig a deep burrow in which the female lays a single egg. When the egg hatches, both parents feed the chick for about six weeks. Then the parents leave the chick alone. After a few days without food, the chick dives into the sea to fish for itself.

The small, graceful Arctic tern is the world's champion animal traveler. It makes a yearly journey around the entire earth, from the Arctic to the Antarctic and back again. During the summer, flocks of terns visit the Arctic to breed and eat small fish along the icy coasts. By early September, the terns begin a two-month trip to the Antarctic, flying over 13,000 miles. They arrive just as summer is beginning in Antarctica and winter is beginning in the Arctic. They feed until it grows cold, then they fly back to the Arctic.

The snowy owl lives in the Arctic all year long. It has a feathery snowsuit that covers its body from head to toe. The feathers are good insulation against the cold. During blizzards, the snowy owl faces right into the wind so that its feathers are pressed against its body and the warmth stays in.

Snowy owls eat small mammals such as mice and lemmings. The female lays about ten eggs and sits on them to keep them warm while her mate brings her food. In about a month, the eggs hatch. The owlets are fed by both parents. Within two months, the owlets are ready to hunt for their own food.

It seems impossible that anything could survive the long months of freezing cold, snow, and winds of a polar winter. But some animals have adapted to this fierce weather. And when the sun returns in the spring, animals once again fill the polar lands, skies, and seas.